In the book page no.	On the CD
I Feel Love	Donna Summer	2	Track 1
I Will Survive	Gloria Gaynor	8	Track 2
I'm So Excited	Pointer Sisters	13	Track 3
Lady Marmalade	LaBelle	20	Track 4
Le Freak	Chic	26	Track 5
Never Can Say Goodbye	Gloria Gaynor	31	Track 6
On The Radio	Donna Summer	40	Track 7
Relight My Fire	Dan Hurtman	48	Track 8
YMCA	Village People	55	Track 9
You Sexy Thing	Hot Chocolate	62	Track 10

International MUSIC Publications

Series Editor: Anna Joyce

Editorial, production and recording: Artemis Music Limited
Design and Production: Space DPS Limited

Published 2001

RESPECT THE VALUE OF MUSIC

Backing

I Feel Love

Words and Music by Giorgio Moroder,
Pete Bellotte and Donna Summer

Backing

I Will Survive

Words and Music by
Frederick Perren and Dino Fekaris

I'm So Excited

Track 3 — Backing

Words and Music by
Anita Pointer, June Pointer,
Ruth Pointer and Trevor Lawrence

Fast and lively

1. To - night's _____ the night _____ we're gon -
(2.) should - n't ev - en think _____
(𝄋) *Instrumental*

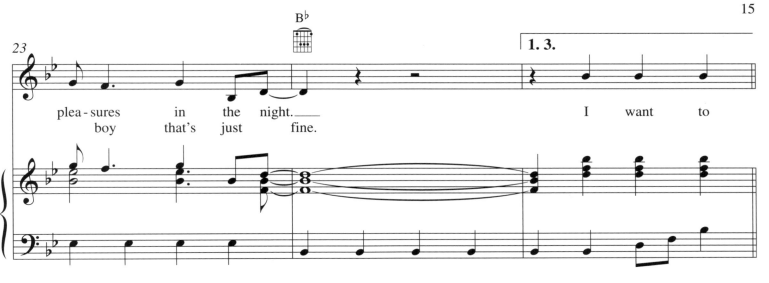

plea-sures in the night.___ I want to
boy that's just fine.

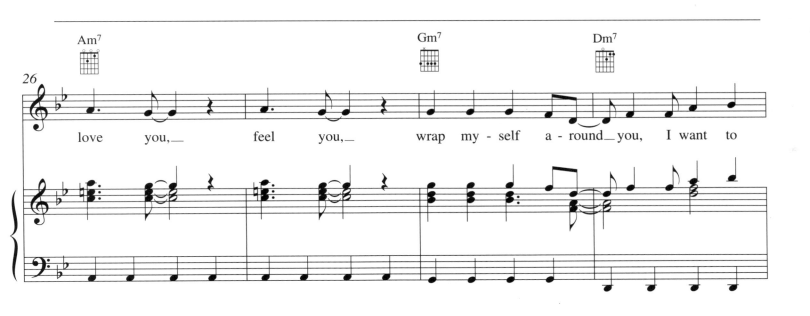

love you,___ feel you,___ wrap my-self a-round___ you, I want to

squeeze you,___ please you,___ I just can't get e-nough,___ and if___ you

Lady Marmalade

Backing

Words and Music by
Bob Crewe and Kenny Nolan

Moderately

Hey sis-ter, go sis-ter, soul sis-ter, go sis-ter. Hey sis-ter, go sis-ter, soul sis-ter, go sis-ter. Met mar-ma-lade,___ down in ol'___ New Or-leans,___

Le Freak

Words and Music by
Bernard Edwards and Nile Rodgers

Never Can Say Goodbye

Backing

Words and Music by
Clifton Davis

ne - ver can say good-bye____ boy.____

On The Radio

Words and Music by
Giorgio Moroder and Donna Summer

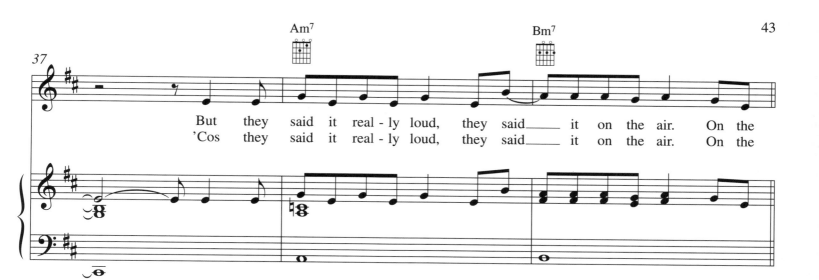

But they said it real-ly loud, they said___ it on the air. On the
'Cos they said it real-ly loud, they said___ it on the air. On the

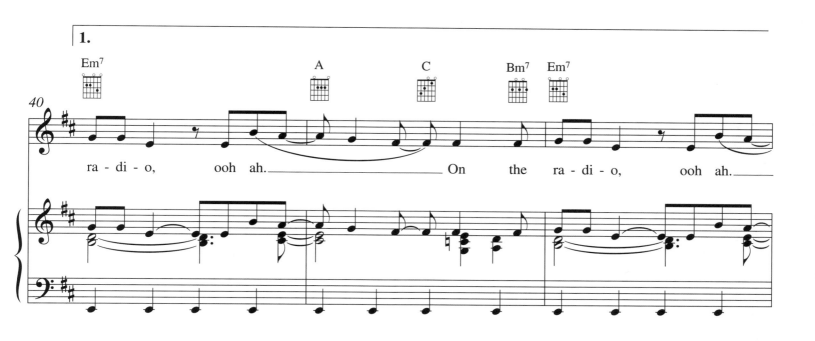

ra - di - o, ooh ah._____ On the ra - di - o, ooh ah.___

_____ On the ra - di - o, ooh ah._____ On the

On the ra - di - o.

Saxophone solo

Relight My Fire

Backing

Words and Music by
Dan Hartman

hope in your soul,___ just keep on walk-ing.

Vocal ad lib.

Strong e-nough___ to walk on through the night,___

there's a new day on the oth-er side,___ and I got

54

Y. M. C. A.

Backing

Moderately brisk

Words and Music by Henri Belolo,
Jacques Moralil and Victor Willis

Young man,   there's no need to feel down.   I said   young man,   pick your-

Young man,   I was once in your shoes.   I said   I was   down and

You Sexy Thing

Words and Music by
Errol Brown

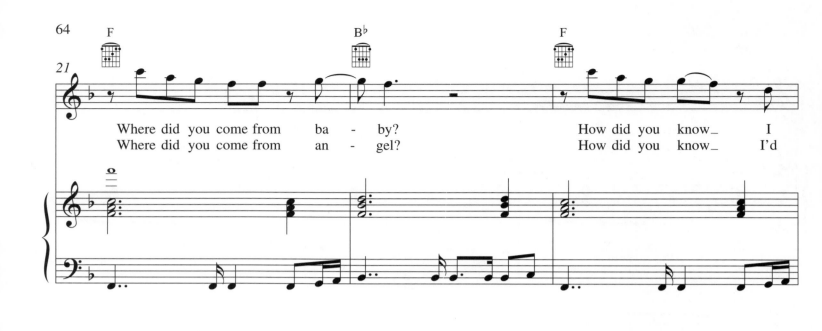

8861A PVC/CD

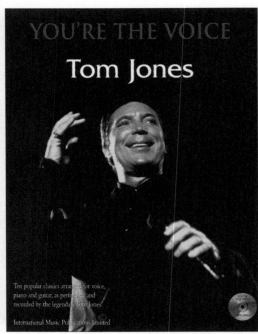

8860A PVG/CD

9297A PVG/CD

Casta Diva from Norma - Vissi D'arte from Tosca Un Bel Di Vedremo from Madam Butterfly - Addio, Del Passato from La Traviata - J'ai Perdu Mon Eurydice from Orphee Et Eurydice - Les Tringles Des Sistres Tintaient from Carmen - Porgi Amor from Le Nozze Di Figaro - Ave Maria from Otello

Delilah - Green Green Grass Of Home - Help Yourself - I'll Never Fall In Love Again - It's Not Unusual - Mama Told Me Not To Come - Sexbomb Thunderball - What's New Pussycat - You Can Leave Your Hat On

Beauty And The Beast - Because You Loved Me - Falling Into You - The First Time Ever I Saw Your Face - It's All Coming Back To Me Now - Misled - My Heart Will Go On - The Power Of Love - Think Twice - When I Fall In Love

COMING SOON: GEORGE MICHAEL

YOU'RE THE VOICE

The outstanding new vocal series from IMP

CD contains full backings for each song, professionally arranged to recreate the sounds of the original recording

ALL SAINTS

6 ▪ **Never Ever**

12 ▪ **Bootie Call**

17 ▪ **I Know Where It's At**

24 ▪ **Under The Bridge**

28 ▪ **Heaven**

34 ▪ **Alone**

39 ▪ **If You Want To Party** (I Found Lovin')

46 ▪ **Trapped**

51 ▪ **Beg**

58 ▪ **Lady Marmalade**

63 ▪ **Take The Key**

68 ▪ **War Of Nerves**

Distributors:
International Music Publications Limited
Southend Road, Woodford Green,
Essex IG8 8HN, England.

International Music Publications GmbH, Germany.
Marstallstraße 8, D-80539 Munchen, Germany.

Nuova Carish S.p.A.
Via Campania, 12 20098 S.Giuliano Milanese (MI)
Zona Industriale Sesto Ulteriano, Italy.
25 Rue D'Hauteville, 75010 Paris, France.

Danmusik, Vognmagergade 7,
DK-1120 Copenhagen K, Denmark.

Warner Chappell Music Australia Pty Limited
3 Talavera Road, North Ryde,
New South Wales 2113, Australia.

Music arranged by Roger Day.
Music processed by Paul Ewers Music Design.
Photos courtesy of London Features International.

Printed in the United Kingdom by
Caligraving Limited, Thetford, Norfolk.

Never Ever

Words & Music by Shaznay Lewis
Music by Rickidy Raw

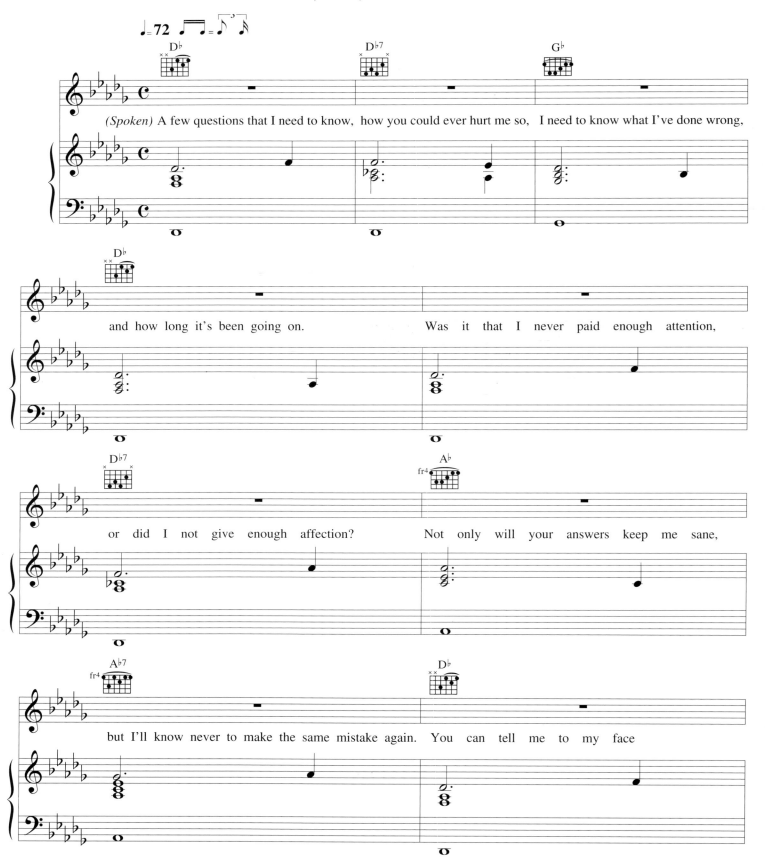

(Spoken) A few questions that I need to know, how you could ever hurt me so, I need to know what I've done wrong, and how long it's been going on. Was it that I never paid enough attention, or did I not give enough affection? Not only will your answers keep me sane, but I'll know never to make the same mistake again. You can tell me to my face

or even on the phone, you can write it in a letter, either way I have to know. Did I never treat you right

did I always start the fight? Either way I'm going out of my mind, all the answers to my questions I have to find.

1. My head's spin - ning, — boy I'm in — a daze, — I feel i - so - lat - ed,
(Verse 2 see block lyric)

don't want to com-mun - i - cate. — I'll take a show-er, I will — scour, — I will run

find peace of mind, the hap - py mind, I once owned _____ yeah.

Flex-in' vo-cab - u - la- ry runs right through me. The al - pha-bet runs right from A to Z.

Con-ver-sa-tions, hes - i - ta- tions in ___ my mind, you got my con-science ask-ing ques-tions that I can't find

I'm not cra - zy. ___ I'm sure I ain't done no-thing wrong. ___ No,

8

I'm just wait - ing, 'cause I heard that this feel-ing won't last___ that long.___

Nev-er ev-er have I ev-er felt so low, when you gon-na take me out of this black hole.

Nev-er ev-er have I ev-er felt so sad. The way I'm feel-ing, yeah you got me feel-ing real-ly bad.

Nev-er ev-er have I had to find, I've had to dig a-way to find my own peace of mind.

Verse 2:
I keep searching deep within my soul
For all the answers, don't wanna hurt no more.
I need peace, got to feel at ease, need to be
Free from pain, go insane, my heart aches.

Sometimes vocabulary runs through my head
The alphabet runs right from A to Z
Conversations, hesitations in my mind.
You got my conscience asking questions that I can't find
I'm not crazy
I'm sure I ain't done nothing wrong
Now I'm just waiting
'Cause I heard that this feeling won't last that long.

Bootie Call

Words & Music by Shaznay Lewis
Music by Karl Gordon

To Coda ⊕

Bring it on, bring it, bring it on now.
(Boo - tie call)

Bring it on, bring it, bring it on now.
(It's just a boo - tie call)

Bring it on, bring it, bring it on now.
(Boo - tie call)

Bring it on, bring it, bring it on now.
(It's just a boo - tie call)

Bring it on, bring it, bring it on now.
(Boo - tie call)

Bring it on, bring it, bring it on now.
(It's just a boo - tie call)

1. Nev - er stop giv - ing good love 'cause that's what I call you for.
(Verse 2 see block lyric)

13

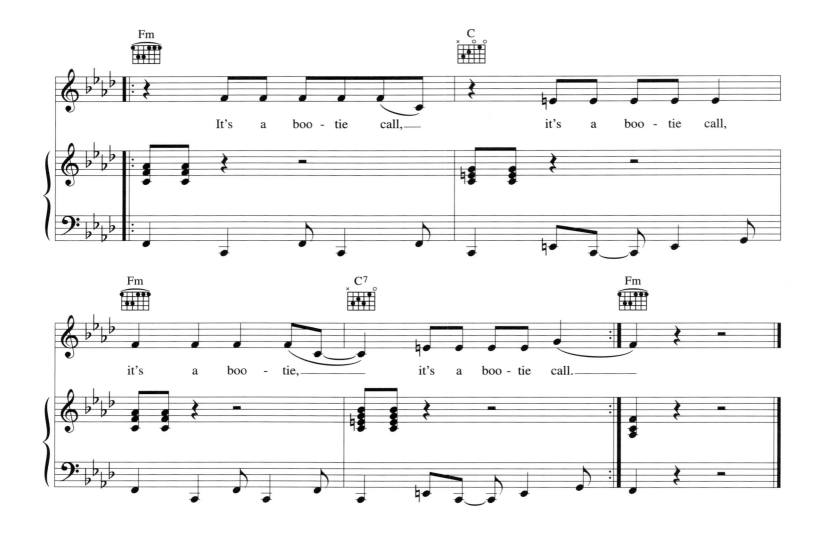

Verse 2:
I'm keen on you what is baby
Some things are always good to have
You never let me down
I'm always happy when you make me laugh
But don't try to find
This heart of mine
Emotions don't come into my head
So don't be misled, my heart doesn't need to be bled.

Only trying to be smart babe
Don't need the rollercoaster ride
I've been and seen and done it all yeah
Don't want you messing with my mind
So don't be a fool
Keep this as your number one rule:
Good loving's not always from the heart
You got to be smart, stay just the way you are.

I Know Where It's At

Words & Music by Shaznay Lewis, Karl Gordon,
Walter Becker, Donald Fagen & Paul Griffin

17

want to have a good time,— if you know you've got some-thing on your

mind,— if you know that you wan-na get on down,— don't de-

-ny it, don't be shy,_____ just come a-round.—

1. I've— been watch-ing you— and I know— you like— to par-ty ba - by,
(Verse 2 see block lyric)

and— you know— that that— sounds real - ly good— to me.—

Ev - 'ry - bo - dy wants— to hang— out at— my par - ty ba - by,

don't— you know— that this— is the on - ly place— to be.—— If you

know that you wan-na get on down,— no need to wor-ry 'cause All Saints will be a-round.—

21

Baby got it goin' on, I don't see nothing wrong, you dance pretty hot and I know you'll like my song,

So move it like that, rat-a-tat-tat, now we'll confirm that you know where it's at. Just come a - round.__ If you

want to have a good time,__ if you know you've got some-thing on your

mind,__ if you know that you wan - na get on down,__ don't de -

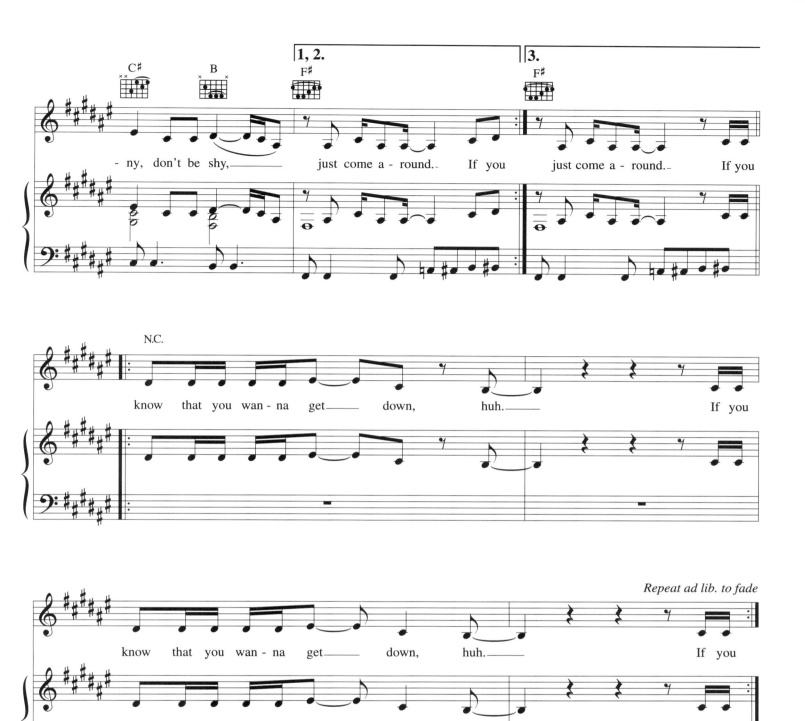

Verse 2:
Move around and get on down, do what you wanna baby,
You gotta be good, you gotta be good and ready to go.
I know you've been waiting for my party all your lifetime baby
Everybody in the whole world wants to know.

Can't you see that there's no-one on the streets
'Cos everybody knows where they've got to be.

Under The Bridge

Words & Music by Anthony Kiedis,
Flea, John Frusciante & Chad Smith

1. Some-times I feel like I don't have a fath-er. Some-times I feel like
(Verses 2 & 3 see block lyrics)

my on - ly — friend. — Is the ci - ty I live — in, the ci - ty of ci - ties,

lone-ly as I am — to - geth- er we — cry, we — cry, we — cry. —

I don't ev - er wan - na feel — like I did that day.
(On 𝄋 vocal ad lib.)

Take me to the place I love, — take me all the way. I don't ev - er wan - na feel —

⊕ *Coda*

Verse 2:

I drive on the streets, 'cause he's my companion
I walk through his fields, 'cause he knows who I am.
He sees my good deeds then he kisses me windy
I never worried, now that is a lie.

Verse 3:

It's hard to believe, there's nobody out there
It's hard to believe that I'm all alone.
At least I have his love, the city he loves me
Lonely as I am, together we cry.

Heaven

Words & Music by Shaznay Lewis, Melanie Blatt,
Natalie Appleton, Nicole Appleton, Cameron McVey & Magnus Fiennes

Lift me up, take me

Verse 2:
Take me high
Above the clouds where the birds fly.
I'm feeling free
Let heaven do the work for me.
Looking over this crazy city
Where we're living
I've seen it, done it
It's just the way I've been.

Bridge (D.%)
I won't fake
I won't break
No way
No.

Alone

Words & Music by Shaznay Lewis
Music by Karl Gordon

real. The — un - hap -

- pi - ness I may — be caus - in' you — — is de - fin - it - ely un - in - ten - tion - al. —

— So — don't hes -

- i - tate, don't be — a - fraid — — to tell me 'cause my ac - tions are not per -

Verse 2:
I need you to be honest, really honest
And tell me what's on your mind.
Whatever the problem may be
You tell me, oh 'cause the body never lies.
Am I too hard, too soft
Or am I really just selfish to the bone?
So don't hesitate, I'm a psychic babe
Let your feelings all be known…
…but I'll tell you something right now.

If You Want To Party (I Found Lovin')

Words & Music by Michael Walker & Johnny Flippin

Hey what's up? Gath-er round, ev-'ry-bo-dy get down, it's time for the best par-ty track in town.

Repeat ad lib. to fade

*Verse 2 (**D.%.**):*
So on and on and on, on and on and on
Check it check it check it out to the break the break of dawn.
Ask the bass drum, stick it to your ear, can you hear?
Move your rear, wind your body to the beautiful snare.
Guys grab a girl and take her from the back
And give it up, give it up, 'cause we like it like that
Girls grab a guy, show him that you ain't feeling shy
Keep it going as the bridge comes back in time.

Trapped

Words & Music by Neville Henry,
Karen Gibbs, Shaznay Lewis & Melanie Blatt

Verse 2:
She looks in the mirror
Her reflection's someone old
Seeing days go by
She don't need to be told.
Feeling a little bit sad
She cries and packs her bags
Remembering a dream
A dream that she'll never have.

Where will she go?
(But it ain't that easy)
How long till she comes home?
(But it's all too sleazy)
Maybe she'll make it
Will she...
...or maybe not.

Beg

Words & Music by Jonathan Douglas, Shaznay Lewis,
John Benson, Ralph MacDonald & William Slater

Lady Marmalade

Words & Music by Bob Crewe & Kenny Nolan

Hey sis - ter, go sis - ter, soul sis - ter, go sis - ter. Hey sis - ter, go sis - ter,

soul sis - ter, go sis - ter. Hey sis - ter, go sis - ter, soul sis - ter, go sis - ter.

(2.) come on and share___ all your deep___ fan - ta - sies,___ I'm
(1.3. spoken see block lyric)

ask - ing, not tell - ing you please,___ Show me all night___ you can do___

Verse 1: (spoken)
Do you fancy enough, hit him in the sack
Yes my kitty cat is a wreck
And then some, you are the one
Gotta represent, gotta go the whole run.
We can play all night, gotta do it right
Snuggle up, huddle up, nice and tight
My place or yours, gotta be raw
Don't really matter once we get through the door.

Verse 3: (spoken)
Mocca chocolata ha
Coucher ce soir
Run, run that's right
Bring it on daddy it's the bedroom fight.
Get ahead, get your drawers and put them on fast
Got to keep up if you think you can last
Gonna get wet, are you ready yet?
On your marks, get set.

Take The Key

Words & Music by Shaznay Lewis
Music by Karl Gordon, Kirk Robinson & Nathaniel Robinson

Verse 2:
Yeah, time stood still
The way I feel would be
Unconditional, eternal, everlasting
Oh you know that I feel complete.

War Of Nerves

Words & Music by Shaznay Lewis, Melanie Blatt,
Natalie Appleton, Nicole Appleton, Cameron McVey & Magnus Fiennes

call my name.

I don't ev-ver want to feel_____ fear,_____ 'cause

ev - 'ry night feels al-right when you're near.

near._

Don't wan - na be like a voice with-out

words.

Don't wan - na be a - lone in this

Verse 2:
Battle through this war of nerves
When your life, it takes a turn
And what I have is what I fear
While in my mind you're lying here.
Feel that unholy dread
There's a piece of me in all he says
All kinds of mixed-up inside my head
This stage fright in my own bed.

At B final choruses:
2
I don't ever want to feel pain
When it's over, will I feel the same?
I don't ever want to feel fear
This war of nerves that I reserve
For when you're here.

3
I don't ever want to feel pain
I'm feeling hurt but I feel no shame
I don't ever want to feel fear
Do I deserve these cruel words
We have here?